Copyright © 2021 by Fareedah Amoo and Kamilah Amoo
Illustrated by Asfand Yar Ashraf

All rights reserved. No part of this publication may be reproduced, distributed, or transmitted in any form, including photocopying, or other electronic mechanical method or means without the prior writing permission of the authors. For Permission requests, solicit the authors via these emails: support@fkakidstv.com , fkakidstv@gmail.com
website: www.fkakidstv.com
Instagram: @fka_kids_tv

Printed in the United State of America

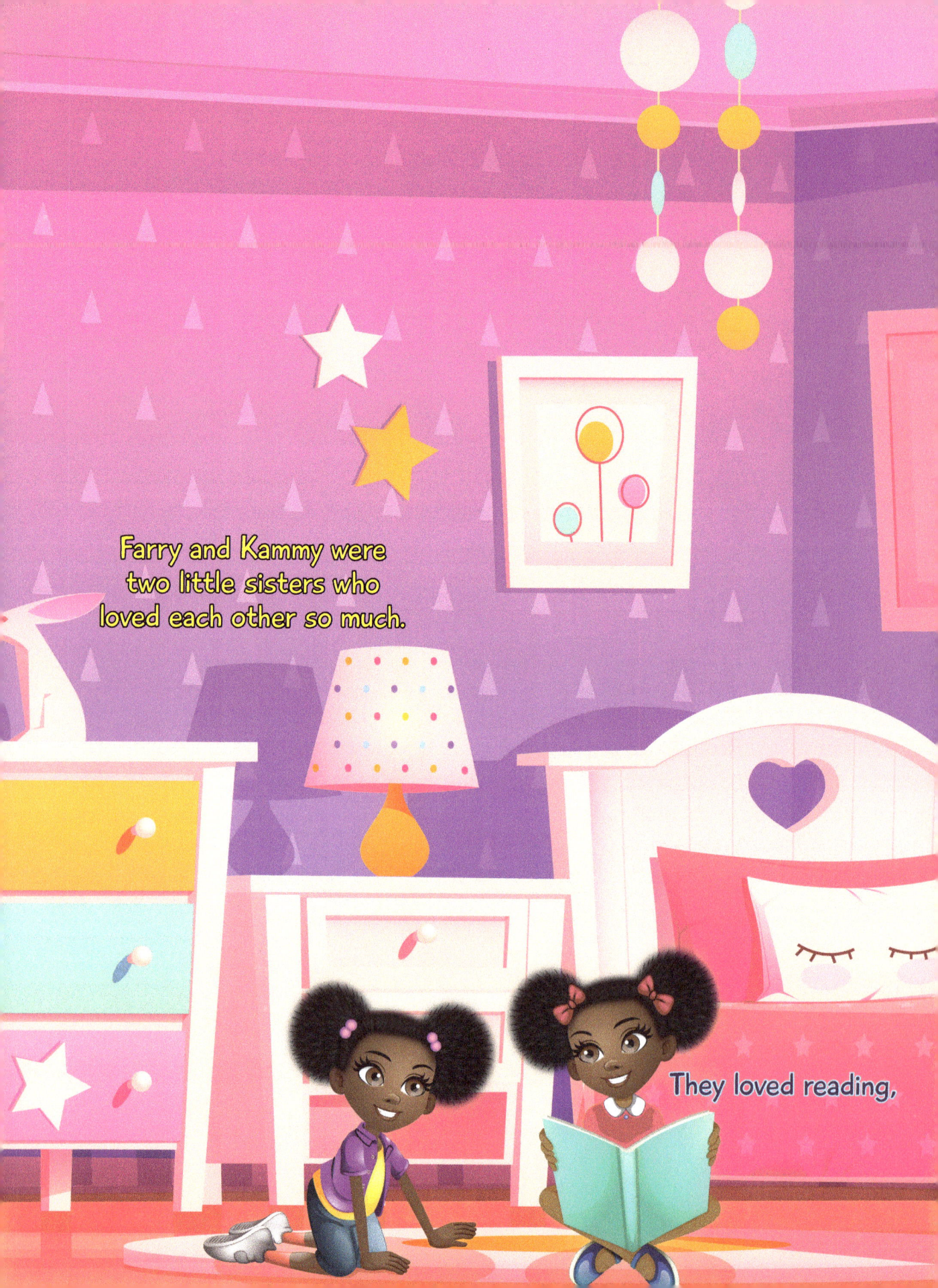

Farry and Kammy were two little sisters who loved each other so much.

They loved reading,

cooking, and baking with Mummy.

and rode bicycles together on the weekends.

Farry and Kammy also liked to play hide and seek with their baby brother, Alan.

THEY WANTED A FOUR-TIER TOWER CAKE.

They started mixing all the ingredients.

They combined every kind of dry magical rainbow cake ingredient they could think of.

Little did they know that they had used more than the portion of ingredients they were supposed to.

After some minutes, the cake started getting BIGGER and BIGGER, and it flooded the house and the street.

Kammy thought they could put the cake on a big plate, but soon she realized she was wrong.

Kammy said, "This is terrible! What are we going to do now?"

The street was full of magical rainbow cake, and the neighbors came out with their children,

and they all started eating, eating, and eating the magical rainbow cake, but it never finished.

"Oh, no, this is out of control!" said Farry.
"This is terrific!" replied Kammy.
"What are we going to do now?"

Farry looked at her little sister. "Hmm..." Kammy asked, "What is it?" Farry said, "I think I know what to do. I think we should use the magical powder to call Fairy Godmother."

They both ran inside the house and used the magic potion to call on the Fairy Godmother.

Godmother arrived and she used her magical power to stop the cake from getting BIGGER, BIGGER, and BIGGER.

Godmother arrived and she used her magical power to stop the cake from getting BIGGER, BIGGER, and BIGGER.

Everyone was tired and sleepy after the beautiful rainy magical rainbow cupcakes; it was already bedtime and Christmas Eve, so the Fairy Godmother sent Farry and her little sister to bed before their parents returned.

The sisters did their bedtime routine: they brushed their teeth, showered, and read their favorite magical books. Then they went to bed.

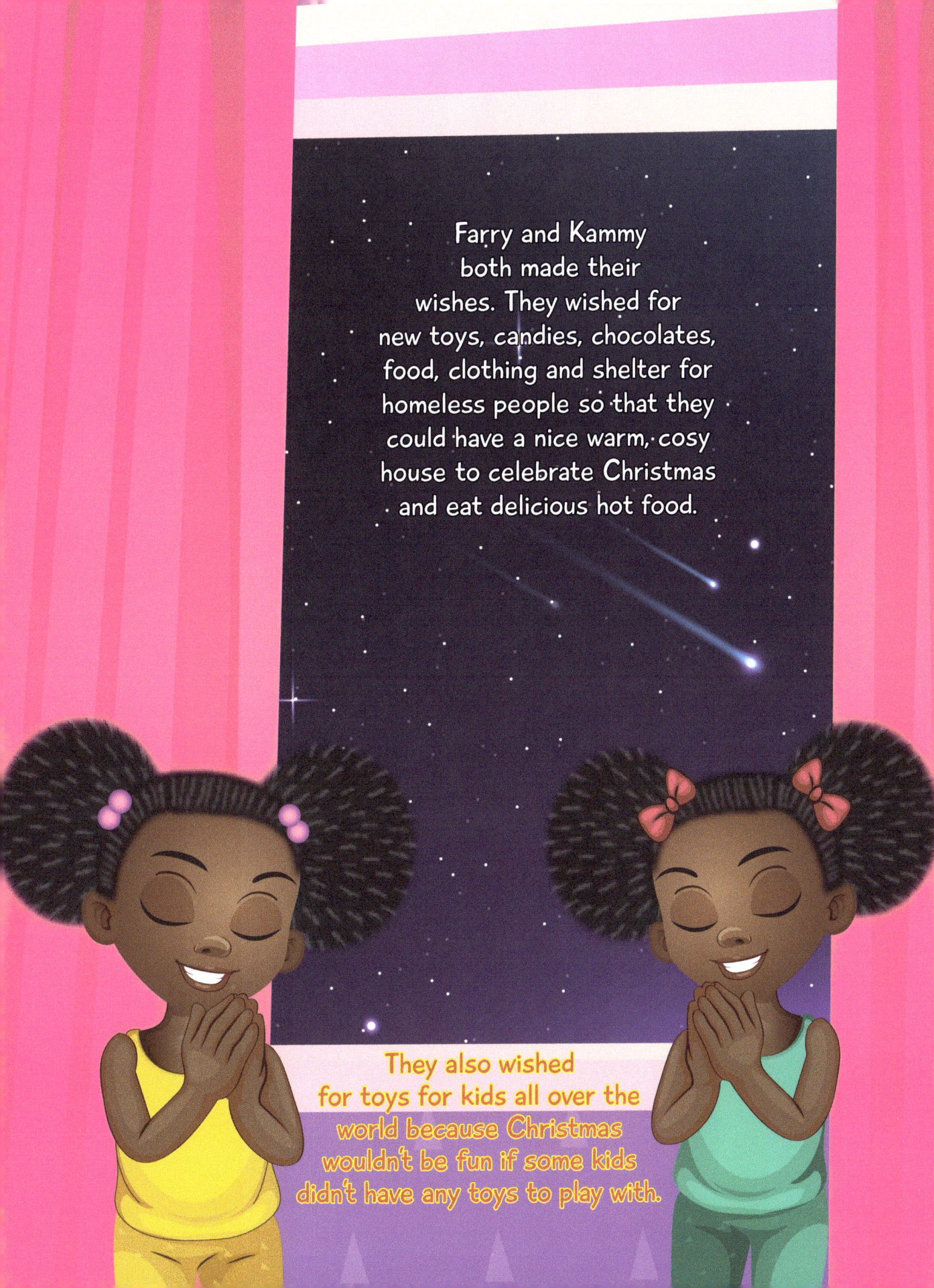

It was Christmas morning, and when the girls woke up, they saw the Fairy Godmother had turned their room into a beautiful, magical wonderland room!

Their beds had been turned into princess castle beds with lots of teddy bears and stuffed animals.

Farry's sleepwear had turned into her favorite character, Wonder Woman's, costume, and Kammy's sleepwear had turned into a Super Girl's costume.

The girls thought they were dreaming and still couldn't believe everything they saw in their room.

Kammy said, "Zoom-zoom!" in her super girl costume. The girls were very happy. They rushed downstairs to tell Mom and Dad what had happened to their room, not knowing that another surprise was waiting for them there.

Mom and Dad said, "SURPRISE!"

Merry Christmas

The girls saw that Santa had dropped plenty of gifts under their Christmas tree for them.

The Fairy Godmother had decorated the whole house; there were lots of gifts and a Christmas tree.

They sat down beside the Christmas tree, and they began to open their gifts. The gifts were all that Farry and Kammy had wished for last night before going to bed and seeing the shooting star.

New toys, a Barbie dream house, chocolate, candy, and bicycles. The Fairy Godmother helped Santa with the gifts.

The girls said, "We are sure that other children across the world have received their gifts, and the homeless people too."

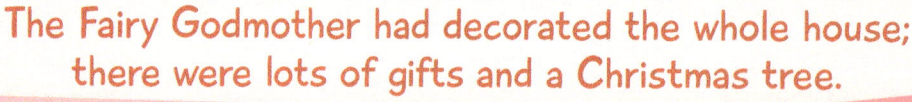

After opening all the gifts, the girls dressed warmly and went outside with their baby brother Alan to play in the snow.

They had a snow fight, made snow angels, made snowballs, made a snowman and used a carrot for his nose, and Farry put her neck warmer on the snowman's neck.

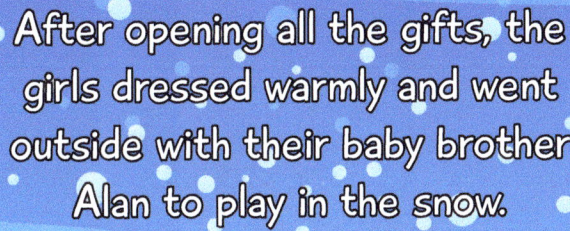

Kammy put her old gloves on the snowman's hands. They made a hideout out of snowballs.

About the Authors

Our names are Fareedah and Kamilah Amoo. We are seven and five year's old sisters and live in Ontario, Canada, with our parents and little brother, Awad.

We love writing stories, painting on canva, coding, reading books, and enjoying arts and crafts. Our goal is to motivate every child worldwide to read more books. We take pleasure in sharing love and kindness with everyone, and that has been our practice since we are babies.

This is our first book, and we will publish more very soon. With this book, we hope to inspire kids worldwide to read more books and believe in themselves. The kids should never stop reading, never stop learning and never stop growing. We love you all. Thank you.

www.ingramcontent.com/pod-product-compliance
Lightning Source LLC
Chambersburg PA
CBHW061123170426
43209CB00013B/1652